# First the Egg

# Laura Vaccaro Seeger

SCHOLASTIC INC.
New York Toronto London Auckland Sydney
Mexico City New Delhi Hong Kong Buenos Aires

# First

# the EGG

then

# the CHICKEN

# First

the TADPOLE

then

# the FROG

# First

# the SEED

then

# the FLOWER

# First

the CATERPILLAR

then

# the BUTTERFLY

th,not?vKnoqeano

qNthenvg;yesDpandk

wow!ifjorkbigzeh,bo

girl;axhowgdownEjrf

l,whoJpaFirstna,that

Can;butAethej!whatfkj

here?goodjn!fbwhe

lsowinogb,qare;where

Ifrom,oh!ptwhyV;badS

rz,jhsWthereohim?

the W██D

# the STORY

Once upon a time
there was an egg
and a chicken and a
tadpole and a frog
and a seed and a
flower and a
caterpillar and a
butterfly and...

First

the PAINT

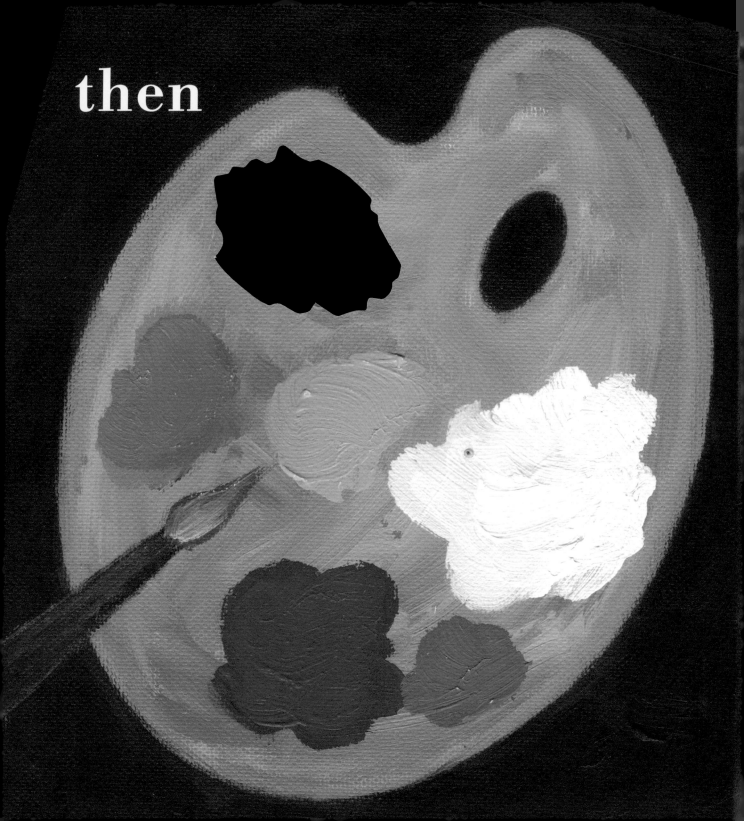

then

the PICTURE . . .

First
the CHICKEN

then

# the EGG!

*for Chris*

ISBN-13: 978-0-545-10550-7
ISBN-10: 0-545-10550-1

12 11 10 9 8 7 6 5 4 3 2 1                    8 9 10 11 12 13/0

Printed in Malaysia                    46

First Scholastic printing, September 2008